THE GREAT RESCUE

Jan Burchett and Sara Vogler

Illustrated by Leo Hartas

Orion
Children's Books

NORTH EAST
LINCOLNSHIRE
LIBRARIES

CLE	LCO
GCL	NUN
GCR	SCO
GRA	SLS
HUM	WAL
IMM 7/13	WIL
LAC	YAR

First published in Great Britain in 2013
by Orion Children's Books
a division of the Orion Publishing Group Ltd
Orion House
5 Upper St Martin's Lane
London WC2H 9EA
An Hachette UK company

1 3 5 7 9 10 8 6 4 2

Text copyright © Jan Burchett and Sara Vogler 2013
Map and interior illustrations copyright © Leo Hartas 2013

The right of Jan Burchett and Sara Vogler to be identified as the authors of this work, and the right of Leo Hartas to be identified as the illustrator of this work have been asserted.

All rights reserved. No part of this publication may be reproduced, stored in a retrieval system, or transmitted, in any form or by any means, electronic, mechanical, photocopying, recording or otherwise, without the prior permission of Orion Children's Books.

The Orion Publishing Group's policy is to use papers that are natural, renewable and recyclable products and made from wood grown in sustainable forests. The logging and manufacturing processes are expected to conform to the environmental regulations of the country of origin.

A catalogue record for this book is
available from the British Library.

ISBN 978 1 4440 0763 3

Printed in Great Britain by Clays Ltd, St Ives plc

NORTH EAST
LINCOLNSHIRE COUNCIL
01030639
Bertrams 10/06/2013
£4.99

For Boris and his six-foot stilts

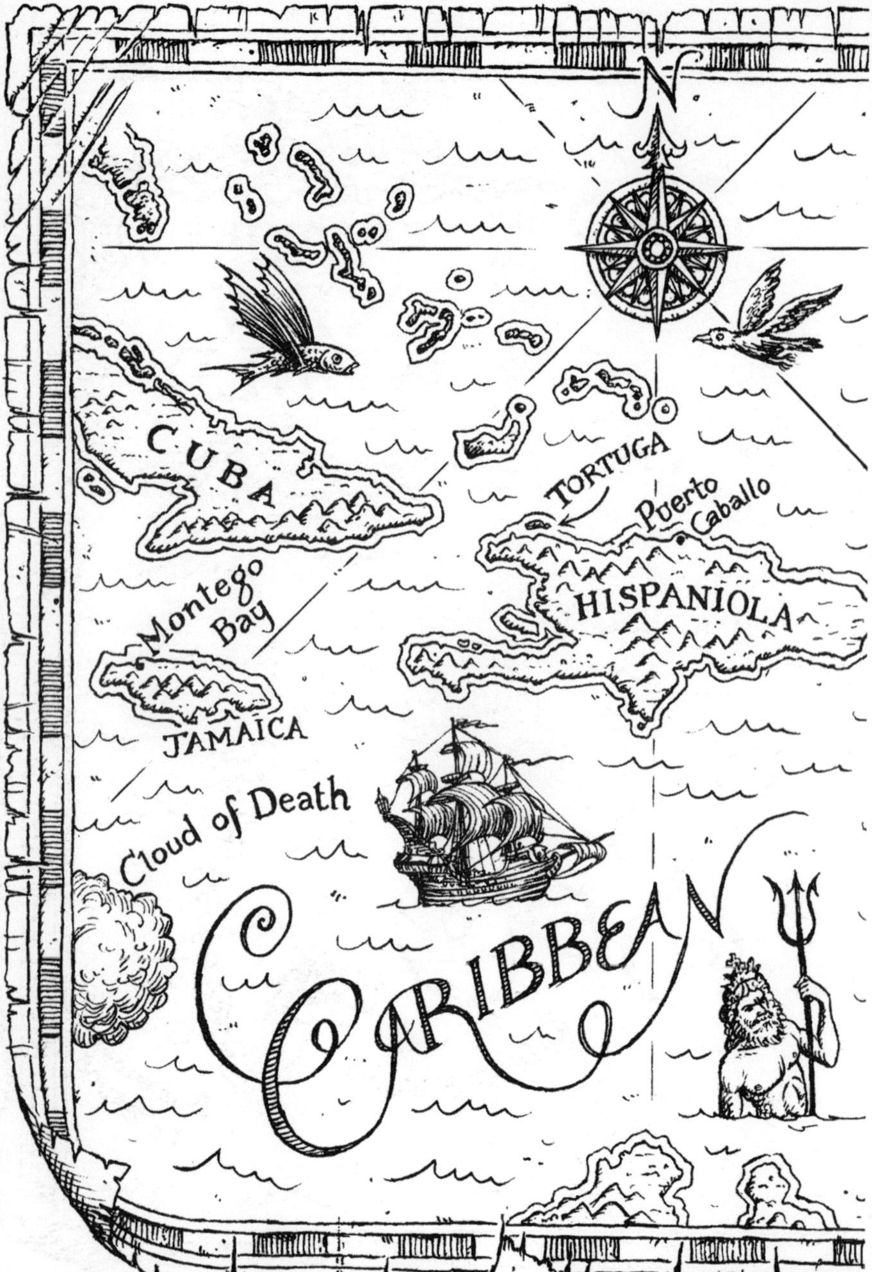

N

CUBA

TORTUGA

Puerto Caballo

HISPANIOLA

Montego Bay

JAMAICA

Cloud of Death

CARIBBEAN

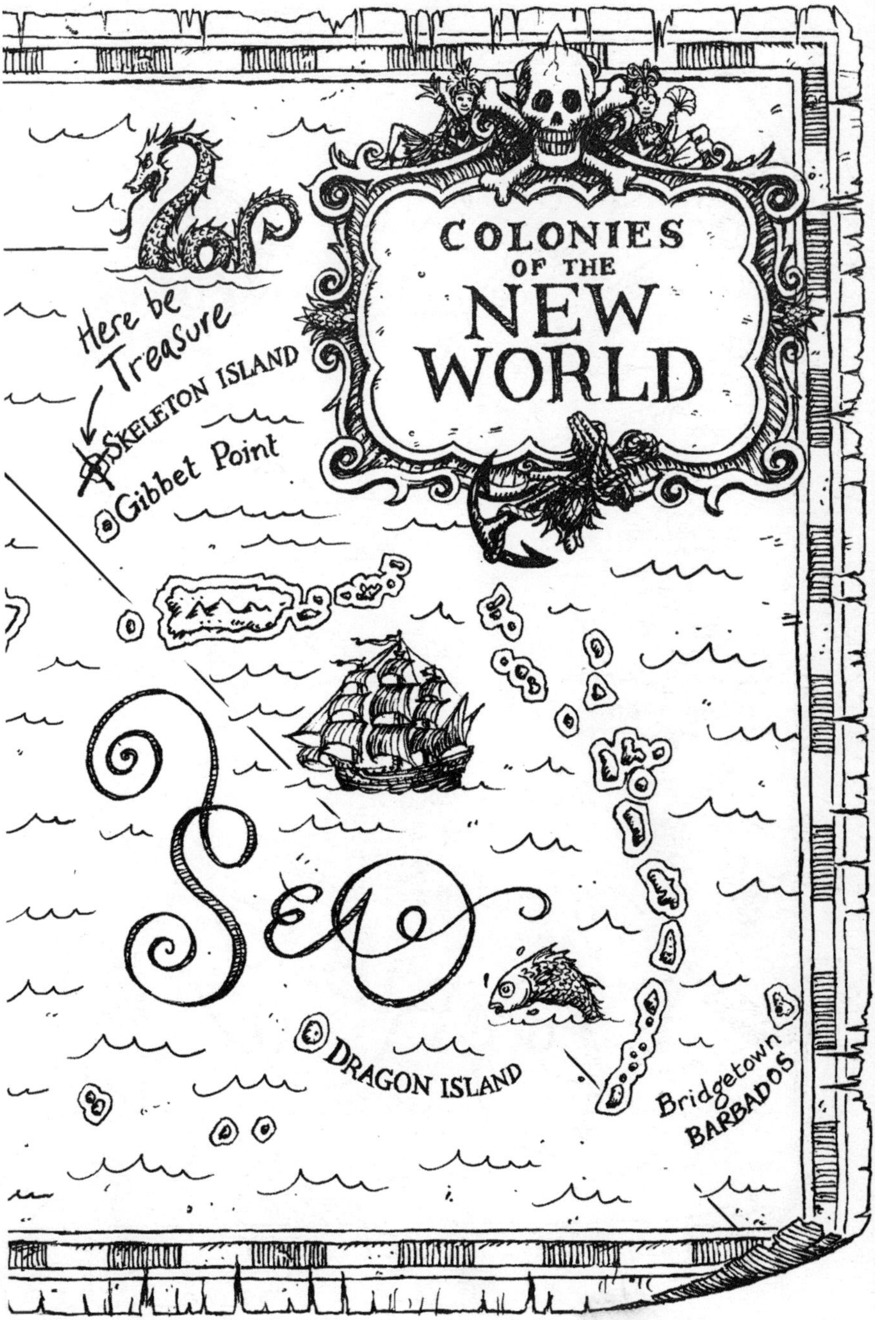

COLONIES OF THE NEW WORLD

Here be Treasure

SKELETON ISLAND

Gibbet Point

Sea

DRAGON ISLAND

Bridgetown

BARBADOS

The SEA WOLF
Captain's Cabin
Hammocks
Gun Deck
Galley
Ship's Stores

Chapter One

Sam Silver stood at his back door, frowning at the stilts in his hands. Why was it so hard to balance on them? The woman at the Circus Skills class had run around the school hall on hers and they'd been really long.

There was only a small concrete yard behind his parents' fish and chip shop, and with no garden it didn't give him much space to practise. But that wasn't going to stop Sam. So far he'd managed three and a half seconds before he'd toppled onto the bins. The noise had brought his father running, a piece of battered cod in his hand. At least Sam had given his dad a good laugh. But he wanted applause. He wanted to be the best stilt-walker in Backwater Bay. Actually he'd be the *only* stilt-walker in Backwater Bay as the Circus Skills woman had only handed out one pair, but that didn't matter.

He stood on an old oil can and grasped the stilts again. He hoisted himself onto them and swayed, leaning against the drainpipe for balance. Then he stepped forward. This time it felt different. He was still upright for a start. He took another step and another, feeling more confident with each one.

"Awesome!" he cried as he staggered

towards the fence. “Eight steps. That must be a world record!”

He swung his leg round to make a turn and at once he realised his mistake. He was spinning too fast. He crashed down on a pile of cardboard boxes, squashing them flat. But he wasn’t going to give up now. Using the washing line, he hauled himself up and set off for the back door, avoiding his mother’s pot plants. This time he made it and leapt down onto the steps in triumph.

"Success!" he yelled up at the seagulls swirling over the bay.

He couldn't wait to show his friend Fernando. Fernando might be an expert juggler but he couldn't walk on stilts. Sam wanted to demonstrate straight away. There was only one problem with this. Fernando lived on a pirate ship in the Caribbean – three hundred years ago. Well, that *would* have been a problem for anyone else, but not for Sam. Sam had a magic doubloon, a gold coin sent to him by an old pirate ancestor, Joseph Silver. He could go back in time whenever he wanted and have an adventure with Captain Blade, Fernando and the bold crew of the *Sea Wolf*. He wouldn't be able to take his stilts as only his clothes time-travelled with him, but there was always spare wood on the ship and he was sure he'd be able to make some.

Sam sprinted up to his bedroom and changed into the old T-shirt and jeans he always wore for his pirate adventures. He didn't have to worry about his parents wondering where he'd gone. The coin would bring him back to exactly the same time in the present as when he left. He grabbed the ancient bottle that stood on his shelf. Tipping out the gold doubloon, he spat on it and gave it a rub. At once, his bedroom walls began to spin around him and he was sucked up into the familiar whirling tunnel that always made him feel he was inside a giant vacuum cleaner. Then everything stopped turning and he landed with a bump on the hard wooden floor of the *Sea Wolf*'s storeroom.

The ship was gently swaying. Sam

jumped up and ran over to a barrel where a jerkin, belt, neckerchief and spyglass were lying. His friend Charlie always made sure they were ready for him when he returned to the past. She was the only one who knew he was from the twenty-first century and even she found it hard to believe. He quickly dressed in his pirate outfit, tucked his spyglass into his belt and left the storeroom ready for action.

The hot midday sun beat down on his head as he bounded up the steps to the main deck. A hearty sea shanty filled the air and when he got to the top of the stairs he saw the crew busy mending sails and splicing rope. Beyond the rail he could see that the ship was at anchor in a quiet bay.

"Sam Silver!" came a surprised shout and Harry Hopp, the first mate, dropped his rope and came stomping over to him, his wooden leg pounding on the deck. He patted him hard on the back, sending Sam staggering. "Shiver me timbers, we're more than a thousand miles away from where we saw you last," he declared, his grizzled face beaming. "How did you get here so quick?"

Sam gulped. When the coin took him back to his own time his shipmates thought he'd just gone off to see his poor widowed mother and help her on her farm. But that wasn't going to explain how he'd managed to whiz across the ocean to be with them when he'd finished milking the cow and mucking out the pig. Speedboats hadn't been invented in 1706!

"He's a true Silver," called Ned the bosun. "Nothing keeps him from his crew."

"Aye!" chorused his shipmates.

Phew! thought Sam. It was useful being descended from a famous pirate. Joseph Silver had been well loved by the pirates and his family could do no wrong.

"By Neptune's trident, we're glad to see you," came a deep voice. A tall man with belts full of weapons and red braids in his beard was striding across the deck to greet him. It was Captain Blade. "With an extra pair of hands we'll have these sails stitched and seaworthy in no time."

Someone gave him a friendly shove from behind. Sam whipped round to find Fernando grinning at him.

"Greetings, my friend," he said, his Spanish accent strong in his excitement at seeing Sam. "Perhaps you could swab the decks instead. Last time you were let loose with a needle you stitched your jerkin to your breeches."

"My sewing's not that bad!" protested Sam. "But wait. I've got something amazing to show you before I start my duties. I'll just find some wood and then . . ."

"Pieces of eight!" A bright green parrot landed on Sam's head and peered down into his face. "Ahoy, me hearty!" he squawked.

"Hello, Crow," said Sam, coaxing the parrot onto his finger.

He saw the captain give the bird a nervous glance so he took Crow away to the side rail. Captain Blade feared no man but he was terrified of parrots. Fernando said it was because a parrot had stolen his favourite teething ring when he was a baby but all the pirates had a different story to tell. Sam was only allowed to keep his feathered friend if everyone pretended he was in fact just a rather brightly-coloured crow.

"So what's this amazing new thing, Sam?" asked Fernando.

"You'll love it," began Sam. "I've learnt how to—"

"Sam!" Charlie came running up,

pushing her bandana back off her forehead. "I'm glad you're here. Wait till you see what Sinbad can do!" Charlie had a mangy black cat draped round her shoulders. Sam and Fernando backed off as he gave them a baleful glare. Sinbad was a loyal crew member but he was quick with his claws if anyone but Charlie tried to touch him.

"I was just about to show—" protested Sam.

"Sinbad's so clever," crooned Charlie, ignoring him. "I've taught him to sing for his supper!" She produced a smelly fish head from her pocket and dangled it in front of the cat's nose. In a flash Sinbad jumped down on the deck, sat bolt upright and set up an ear-piercing wail. Everyone blocked their ears in horror until Charlie threw the fish head down and he devoured it in two gulps.

"What do you think?" said Charlie in delight.

"Very good," answered Sam shakily. "Or it would be if he could keep the volume down." He brightened up. "Time for my trick at last. You'll be so impressed—"

TWA-ANG! There was a strange whistling sound and an arrow thudded into the mast, narrowly missing the captain's head.

"We're under attack!" cried Fernando.

Chapter Two

Crow gave a shriek of alarm and flew to the top of the mainmast.

"Man the starboard cannon!" cried Harry Hopp, leading a team of pirates down the steps to the gun deck. "Arrows are no match for balls of lead."

The crew rushed to fetch powder and cannonballs.

"Arm yourselves," yelled Ben Hudson,

the quartermaster. He was handing out cutlasses to the men as they passed. "We don't know who we're dealing with."

His heart thumping, Sam rushed to get a sword, then joined Fernando at the nearest cannon. He opened a keg of gunpowder.

"Belay that!" bellowed the captain suddenly. "We'll not be needing any weapons."

Everyone turned to gawp at him. Blade was holding the arrow in his hand, unwinding a piece of cloth tied tightly to the shaft. Sam could see it had a strange symbol painted on it. It looked like a knobbly spider.

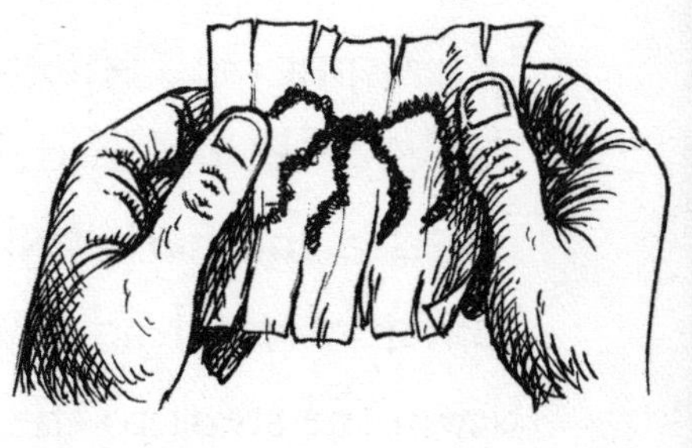

The captain turned to survey the shore. "This is no attack," he said. "It's a message and I know who sent it – my old friend

Chief Madal of the Layakati. I recognise his mark."

Ben called down to the gun deck and Harry Hopp and his men came surging up the steps to see what was going on.

"Who are the Layakati?" asked Sam.

"Well, I'll be a haddock in a hammock!" exclaimed Ned, giving him a curious glance. "I thought you'd have heard of them, lad."

Oh dear, thought Sam. *I forgot I'm meant to know the Caribbean as well as the rest of the crew do.*

"The Layakati people have lived on this coast for as long as anyone can remember," Harry put in. "Their village is on the banks of Lake Laya, the big lagoon a few miles inland from here."

"Oh, yes . . . of course . . ." stammered Sam. "The *Layakati.* I thought you said the, er, Laya . . . *plati.*"

"Stap me!" said Harry, scratching his bald head. "I've never met any tribe of that name."

"Nor have I," agreed Sam.

"I owe my life to Chief Madal and his people," Captain Blade told him. "I would have died of fever if it hadn't been for their shaman and his wonderful medicines. I'll warrant Madal has seen our ship and is inviting us to a feast." He looked keenly towards the shore.

At that moment a boy stepped out of the trees, waved furiously and swiftly disappeared back into the forest.

"That is Usiano, Madal's son," said Captain Blade, pulling thoughtfully at the braids in his beard. "This is very strange. Why is he on his own? I must go ashore. I sense my friend is in trouble."

"He looked scared," said Fernando.

"Be careful, Captain," warned Harry. "We have enemies who would stop at nothing to lure us into a trap. They could be using that innocent young boy as bait."

The captain gave a brief nod. "It is

possible, but I'll not turn my back on my friends." He put the arrow in his belt. "Fernando, Sam, Charlie, come with me. Ben and Ned, too." The captain chose more men, enough to fill the two rowing boats. "The rest stay on watch for signs of danger."

"We'll load those cannon after all," grunted Harry.

"Cutlasses at the ready," ordered Blade in a low voice as they pulled the boats up the sandy beach.

Sam looked back at the *Sea Wolf.* Her guns were aimed at the shore. Sam's mouth felt dry. He wondered who could be watching in the trees, waiting for them.

Keeping low, the pirates moved stealthily up the beach towards the forest.

"Usiano appeared over there," murmured Fernando, pointing to the thickest undergrowth a little further along.

They heard a faint rustle among the leaves and crouched, ready for attack.

"Don't move until I tell you, men," whispered their captain. "As Harry said, this may be a trap."

"Captain Blade!" came a frightened voice. "It is I, Usiano." The words were English but spoken with a strange accent.

A boy emerged slowly from among the tree trunks. He was about Sam's age with long dark hair, held by a patterned band. His feet were bare and he wore knee-length trousers made of animal skin. He carried a long, slender bow.

That looks awesome! thought Sam. The only time he'd ever got his hands on a bow and arrow was when he'd made one with canes taken from his dad's tomatoes. Unfortunately, the tomatoes had fallen down and he'd broken a window with the arrow.

"Come to the shelter of the trees," hissed Usiano. We may be seen if we stay in the open."

The pirates didn't move.

"This is not a trap, Captain," said Usiano. "I swear it by the great spirit Hallucca."

"That's good enough for me," declared Blade. "To the trees, men."

Eyes darting all around, the pirates followed the boy to the cover of the forest undergrowth.

"I am so glad that you are here, Captain Blade!" said Usiano, and Sam could hear the relief in his voice. "I was ready to sail the great sea to find you. I prayed that you would come to us – and my plea was heard."

"What's wrong?" asked Blade. "Tell me quickly."

"You are a good friend to my people, yes?" said Usiano.

"You know that's true," replied the captain, putting his hand on the boy's shoulder. "I owe them my life."

"Then I am pleading for your help," the boy went on in a rush. "My people are in terrible danger."

"Where is your father?" asked Blade. "Why hasn't he come with you?"

The boy gulped and his eyes filled with tears. "I believe he is dead."

Chapter Three

"How can my friend be dead?" gasped Captain Blade. "What happened?"

"Our village has been invaded," said Usiano. "My people have been taken prisoner."

"Was it another tribe?" demanded Fernando.

"No," said Usiano. "The men were foreign like you and they had guns."

"How did they overcome your people, lad?" asked Blade. "I thought your father always set guards."

"He did," said Usiano. "I do not understand why they failed us. They are good warriors. We were having a feast to mark my twelve years of life. My father had given me this new bow and I was about to try it out."

"And that's when the invasion happened?" put in Ned.

Usiano nodded. "Suddenly we were surrounded by armed men. They came crashing from the forest, shouting and pushing us. I saw my father and our tribesmen trying to resist but they had no chance without weapons. Women snatched up their children and ran away but they were all caught and forced back into the village. I managed to slip into the water and hide among the reeds – luckily I still had hold of the bow and this one arrow."

He gulped. "I think I was the only one to escape."

Sam shuddered at the horrible tale. He could imagine how frightened this boy must feel – yet he hadn't given up trying to save his people.

"And your father?" Blade asked Usiano.

"He was bound and dragged off to much jeering from our captors," said Usiano. "They said they were going to kill him."

The crew muttered angrily.

"The invaders made it clear what they were seeking," the boy went on bitterly. "You remember, Captain, how rich our lagoon is in oysters."

Blade nodded. "And every one producing a magnificent pearl."

"They said my people must find pearls for *them* now," said Usiano. "They have been made into slaves and these evil men will sell the pearls to make themselves rich."

"They must be mercenaries," said Ned.

"Evil men like that will do anything for money." He turned and spat.

"You are right," replied Usiano. "As soon as I could, I swam away. I knew I needed to find help for my village and I thought of you, the captain and brave crew of the *Sea Wolf*."

"We'll not let you down," said Blade gruffly, taking Usiano's arrow from his belt and handing it to him. "Your people saved my life and I always pay my debts. Let us be thankful they are being kept alive – if only as miserable slaves. We'll delay no more."

Usiano's eyes shone. "Follow me."

He headed into the trees, forging a path through the thick undergrowth.

Sam bounded after him, glad he was wearing his trainers on the tangle of twigs and thorns of the forest floor. "You're really brave, Usiano!" he said in admiration.

"I am the chief's son," Usiano replied simply. "I have to help my people. You would do as much, I am sure."

"I don't know about that," said Sam. "The only time my home was invaded was when my Auntie Tanya came round with her three-year-old triplets. I legged it over the back fence."

Usiano gave him a strange look, but at that moment Charlie ran up to join them.

"You two were not with the crew when they last came to my village," said Usiano.

"I'm Sam and this is Charlie," said Sam. "We haven't been on the *Sea Wolf* long."

Usiano looked at Sam for a moment. "You wear strange things," he said at last.

"He's not from round here," said Charlie quickly. "In fact, everything's different where he comes from."

"I see," said Usiano, staring at the racing car on Sam's T-shirt.

"And I don't expect you've met a girl

pirate before," Sam burst out before Usiano had a chance to ask what it was. "Charlie ran away from her horrible stepfather. She's as brave as any boy."

"I am glad to hear it," Usiano told Charlie, "for you will need to be if we are to win my village back."

Sam had never been anywhere like this before. There weren't any rainforests in Backwater Bay. The trees towered over their heads and the plants were huge and twisted into ugly shapes. It reminded him of the pictures in fairy tales he'd read when he was little.

It was hard going as the hours passed. The dense treetops blocked out the sun but the air was hot and steamy. Sam wiped his wet forehead. This was even worse than working in the fish and chip shop on a busy Friday night. Every now and then bursts of warm rain trickled down through the thick forest canopy. Insects buzzed around their heads and the trees were filled with the calls of animals and birds. A flock of macaws took to the air in a flutter of scarlet feathers as the pirates passed.

A sudden breeze blew up, shaking the branches and splattering the crew with drops of water.

"Is your village in the middle of the forest?" Sam asked Usiano.

"It is built in a clearing on the shores of Lake Laya," said the boy over his shoulder. "It is beautiful . . . well, it was. I do not know what will await me on my return."

"You speak very good English," said Charlie.

"We have long traded our pearls with your sailors," explained Usiano. "It is sensible for us to know your language."

"Do you get lots of pearls from your oysters?" asked Sam. The only shellfish he'd ever seen were the cockles and mussels that were sold in the harbour in Backwater Bay.

"We fish carefully," said Usiano. "If we take all the oysters at once then they cannot breed and there will be no more. I fear that these men will empty our lagoon, leaving us nothing."

"That sort of thing's still happening where I come from," said Sam. "I heard something about it on *News Talk* last night."

"Sam!" came Charlie's warning voice and he realised Usiano had turned to stare at him, puzzled.

"I mean . . . I heard someone I *knew* talk about it last night," he went on quickly.

Wheep! Wheep! A piercing cry echoed above their heads, sounding like a car alarm and making Sam jump.

"It's only a bird," said Usiano. "Your captain calls them mockingbirds but my people believe that some spirits use creatures of the forest to talk to us. This one is troubled by the danger my tribe is facing."

Suddenly the air was full of birds' warning screeches. Monkeys leapt away through the branches, shrieking in panic. The whole forest seemed to be alive with terror.

"Something's coming!" gasped Fernando.

Chapter Four

An ear-splitting wail cut through the air and a furious ball of matted black fur landed in front of them.

"What devil spirit is this?" cried Usiano.

"It's Sinbad!" exclaimed Charlie in delight. "Our lovely ship's cat. He must have swum ashore to find us."

The lovely ship's cat plonked himself down in front of her, eyeing the crew with pure venom. Then he opened his mouth and wailed again.

"Bless his little heart," crooned Charlie as the crew staggered back, covering their ears. "He just wants his dinner." She pulled a squashed sardine from her pocket and threw it to Sinbad. It was gone in a flash. She picked him up and draped him round her shoulders. He nuzzled into her neck, purring loudly.

Usiano grinned. "It still looks like a devil spirit to me," he whispered to Sam.

"You're right there!" answered Sam. "Just

be glad he's on our side."

Usiano set off again, leading the way through a tangle of creepers. The crew hurried to keep up, slashing at the sticky tendrils that wrapped themselves round their feet.

"Look at that," gasped Charlie, pointing at a blackened tree with a hollow trunk and dead, twisted branches hanging so low that they almost touched the forest floor. "It's like a giant spider!"

"It is the tree of Hallucca," whispered Usiano. "Hallucca is the most powerful

spirit in the forest and that is his home."

"That tree was on the cloth you sent to the captain!" exclaimed Sam.

Usiano nodded. "It is the symbol of our people. I knew Captain Blade would recognise it."

A gust of wind shook the leaves above their heads and an eerie echo sounded round the forest.

"Hallucca speaks," said Usiano in a low voice.

Sam could see that the pirates were looking scared. And he could understand why. The sound was very creepy. He didn't believe it was really this Hallucca, but what on earth was it?

He felt the wind grow stronger and as it blew, the noise swelled.

"Are you sure it's your Hallucca?" croaked Ben. "It sounds more like a ghost to me."

"Aye, a ghost who wants us gone," whispered Ned.

"Or a soul in torment," gasped Fernando, making the sign of the cross.

Usiano turned to face them. "Listen to me," he said. "Hallucca means you no harm. He is bewailing the plight of my village. He is glad that you are here to rescue my people."

"And rescue them we will!" declared Captain Blade.

"Aye, lad," said Ned stoutly. "We won't let you down."

"Spooks don't scare us," added Fernando, although Sam could see he'd turned pale.

Usiano smiled. "I am grateful to you all." He bowed to the dead tree, his hands across his chest. "I will lead you to my village now – and let Hallucca be."

The pirates moved forwards in a tight bunch behind Captain Blade, jostling each other along as if they were all trying to get into the middle of the pack. Their eyes were everywhere, scanning the treetops and bushes.

Is there really an angry spirit around? thought Sam, with a shiver. *Perhaps angry spirits really did exist three hundred years ago. The pirates certainly believe in them.*

Another gust of wind shook the leaves around them and the eerie wailing came again. And all of a sudden, Sam knew what it was! The sound they could all hear was the wind blowing through the hollow tree and making this unearthly moan, but he couldn't tell the crew that. They wouldn't believe him and Usiano might think he was mocking the spirit. He saw Charlie's anxious face. He could tell her – at least she would understand and not be worried any more.

He pulled her back, avoiding Sinbad's flashing claws.

"What are you doing?" she said, trying to shake him off. "We don't want to lose the others with that scary spirit around."

"It's not a scary spirit," said Sam in a low voice.

Charlie looked at him. "Are you sure?" she said, glancing nervously over her shoulder. "I could almost believe the tree was a real spider and that howling was like my worst nightmare."

"That's just the wind blowing through the dead trunk," Sam explained.

Charlie thought for a moment. "I hope you're right," she said at last. "Usiano's people think it's a spirit – and so do all the crew!"

"I know it sounds really spooky,"

admitted Sam, "but it's not. You have to believe me. It's a bit like when my uncle tries to play the didgeridoo he got in Australia. He blows into a hollow tube and a horrible sound comes out. It always frightens my mum."

Charlie gawped at him. "Didgeridoo . . . Australia . . . What are you talking about?" she demanded.

"Sorry," said Sam. He'd forgotten that no one in 1706 would have heard the name Australia. "You'll know in about seventy years."

They caught up with the others, but they hadn't gone very far when Usiano motioned for them to stop again.

"My village is there," he told them.

He pointed ahead. Beyond the trees, they could see glimpses of wooden huts surrounding a clearing. The huts had rough thatched roofs and were built on posts that raised them off the ground.

To Sam they looked like the beach huts at Backwater Bay with little wooden steps up to the doors – except that these huts didn't have pink holidaymakers in socks and sandals inside, boiling up tea.

Usiano turned to Captain Blade, frowning anxiously. "I cannot see what is happening to my people from here. I will go closer."

"We need to know how many mercenaries there are and how they are positioned," said the captain, nodding. "But one pair of eyes cannot spy on the whole village. Take Fernando and Sam with you."

"We will have to go high in the trees to get a good view," said Usiano, looking doubtfully at the boys.

"These two are well used to climbing the ship's rigging," Captain Blade assured him. "They'll have no trouble in these trees."

Usiano smiled at the boys. "Of course – and the more eyes the better we shall see. But we must make no sound or we will be discovered."

Sam felt a rush of fear stab at him like a knife. The invaders sounded merciless. If they were caught, he didn't want to think what the men might do to him and his crewmates.

Chapter Five

Sam and Fernando followed Usiano as he crept through the undergrowth. They came to the edge of the clearing where they could see a few huts. Women in tunics were squatting in front of them, cooking over open fires. They did not speak to each other but glanced about nervously as a surly-looking man in tattered trousers and a dirty shirt strutted among them, pistol at the ready. He stopped pacing and leaned idly against a small enclosure full of goats, to watch his prisoners.

"I don't remember your people keeping goats," whispered Fernando.

"We don't," said Usiano. "The men must have brought them for their food. We live off the creatures of the water and the forest," he told Sam. "The lagoon floods every year in the rainy season and those poor beasts would drown there."

"So that's why you have your homes up on posts," said Sam. Then he noticed a low, domed tent made of animal skins and covered in feathers and shells. The spidery tree emblem hung over the door. "Except for that one."

"That belongs to Nakili, our shaman, you would say 'wise man', I think," explained Usiano. "When the floods come, he gives his home to the lagoon and builds a new one."

An elderly villager came into sight, dragging a heavy bundle of logs. He stumbled, hardly able to walk, and the surly man came over and kicked him.

"That is Nakili himself," gasped Usiano. "If they will treat a shaman in this way, what might they do to the rest of my people?"

"They are heartless!" murmured Fernando. "And the sooner we work out how to overcome them, the better."

"We should spread out," said Usiano.

"We will see more. Fernando, you take that pine tree. Sam, this cedar will give you a good view, and I will go a little further round. Between us, we should be able to see the whole village."

Sam swung himself up into the tree and climbed until he reached a high, swaying branch, hidden by dense leaves. The tree was covered in thick vines that hung down in great loops like green tinsel. He spotted Fernando in a tree nearby and gave him a thumbs-up. He couldn't see Usiano. He must be camouflaged by the forest canopy. The late afternoon sun was casting deep shadows over the village. Beyond the nearest huts he could now see that the settlement was on the bank of a wide lagoon. Out on the water, mercenaries sat in canoes. The tribesmen were diving and surfacing with round dark shells in their hands. Their guards snatched the shells greedily and threw them into buckets, poking the divers with pistols if they were too slow with their work. Sam leaned out as far as he could to check out the bank of the lagoon. There were no guards on the shore at all. He must remember to tell the captain.

Something slid across his hand. He looked down and just managed to stop himself from yelling out in fear. A yellow snake with vivid brown markings was slithering along the branch. He didn't know much about snakes but the markings were like the adder he'd seen once in Backwater Wood. He was pretty sure that, like the adder, that meant this one was poisonous too. The snake stopped, its tongue darting out over his arm. Perhaps it would move on in a minute if he kept perfectly still. But he wasn't sure he could do that. The branch was swaying in the breeze and it was hard to balance. He felt his hand slip.

The snake slowly raised its head, making a tall swaying S shape with its long thin body. Sam realised with horror that it was about to strike. Without thinking, he threw himself at a vine that hung close by. As he tumbled down, his hands closing round the strong vine stem, he heard the hiss of the snake lashing out. He'd escaped just in time, but now he was swinging helplessly, smashing through leaves and branches.

It looks much easier in the Tarzan films! he thought as twigs caught at his skin, leaving stinging scratches.

He crashed into a thick branch and the vine was whipped from his grasp. Flinging out his arms, he dug his fingers into the rough bark to stop himself from falling, then swung his legs up and hooked them round the branch.

Suddenly there was a loud crack. The branch was breaking under his weight. In

a split second he imagined the ground rushing up to meet him. Then his ankles were suddenly caught in a strong grasp. He swung helplessly.

"Perhaps you shouldn't eat so many ship's biscuits, my friend," hissed Fernando. "You are getting too heavy to hold!"

He pulled Sam to safety.

"Thanks," he gasped.

Fernando had a huge grin on his face. "You reminded me of a terrified raccoon!" he chuckled. "It was nice of you to drop in, but you could have been a bit quieter!"

"I was escaping from a snake," explained Sam. "I'm just glad that the mercenaries didn't hear me."

Fernando stiffened. "I'm not so sure they didn't," he muttered.

They could hear shouts. The mercenaries were on their way. They were going to be discovered!

Chapter Six

Sam and Fernando frantically pulled themselves along the branch, towards the dense leaves that would hide them. But down below, mercenaries were running to their tree, shouting and waving their guns.

A deafening shriek suddenly filled the air. Sam twisted round until he could see where the sound was coming from. It was Usiano, perched in his tree, his hands cupped over his mouth. Sam went cold at the sight. It looked as if the boy was signalling to their enemy. Had he led them into a trap after all? Maybe he wasn't the friend that the captain thought he was!

Before Sam could think what to do, Usiano made the shrill cry again.

"Monkeys," growled one of the guards. "They're always crashing about in the trees. Keeps me awake all night sometimes. I'd shoot them if I had my way."

The men turned and headed back to the village.

Sam felt silly. Of course Usiano hadn't been signalling. He was saving them from being discovered. As soon as the mercenaries were out of earshot he and Fernando shinned down the tree.

"Thanks," Sam said as Usiano ran to join them. "You saved our lives."

Usiano wasn't listening. He was peering intently at the village that could just be seen through the thick undergrowth.

"It *is* him," he murmured. "I thought I saw him just now."

"Who?" demanded Fernando.

"My uncle Adisman," said Usiano eagerly, pointing to a figure crouched by a post of one of the huts. "He is my father's younger brother. I am so pleased he is still alive."

The man was scooping water up from an earthenware pot and drinking. A guard strode up and down nearby.

"I must let him know we are here," said Usiano. "The moment that guard has his back turned, I will send him my arrow."

He drew back the string of his bow and waited until the mercenary was walking away. Then he let the arrow fly. It whizzed through the air and landed with a small thud in the post, just above his uncle's head.

Adisman jumped, nearly knocking the pot of water over. Then he seemed to recognise the arrow. He peered in the direction of its flight, urgently scanning the trees. As the guard turned to stride back towards him he pulled the arrow from the wood, threw it down behind him and kicked earth over it. The man approached and they could see him speak. Adisman kept his head bowed as he replied.

"Did the guard see the arrow?" gasped Sam.

"I think not," said Usiano in relief as the man walked away at last.

As soon as he was gone, Adisman threw himself to the ground and scuttled under the hut to reach the thick undergrowth beyond it. They could see him skirting the village, making his way towards their position.

Sam, Fernando and Usiano ran to tell the pirates what had happened.

"My uncle is coming," said Usiano. "Let me greet him alone. He is a nervous man who has never been strong. He will be frightened to see so many at once."

"We'll stay back," agreed Blade.

They could hear furtive movements in the nearby bushes. Usiano stepped out of sight to greet his uncle.

They heard a gruff voice speaking rapidly in a language they did not understand.

"I am sorry to have caused you such pain, Uncle," came Usiano's reply in English, "but how could I let you know I was free? Now I have brought help. You remember Captain Blade and his crew."

There was a pause.

"Where are they?" asked Adisman. "How many have come?"

Blade went forward slowly, his crew

keeping their distance behind him. "We are here, and we will do all we can to rid you of these villains."

Sam watched as Adisman stared round wide-eyed at the pirates. Then his wary face broke into smiles and he gave Usiano a huge hug.

"I prayed to the spirits that you had been spared," he said.

"But what happened to my father?" asked Usiano anxiously.

For a moment Adisman looked away, then he turned back to his nephew, his eyes full of tears. "You must be brave," he said gently. "Your father is dead."

Usiano stood stock still, staring ahead as he heard what he'd feared for many days.

Captain Blade put a hand on the boy's shoulder.

"That is grave news," he said. "He was a loyal friend."

Adisman studied the *Sea Wolf*'s captain for a moment. "I remember you," he said. "Nakili nursed you back to health, many summers ago."

"That's right," Blade nodded. "And I'll not stand by and see your people wronged."

"The best thing you can do is to keep my nephew safe," said Adisman. "He is the last of the direct line. Take him far from here. I would take him myself but I have a wife and children in the village and I cannot leave them. I ask you, Captain, to save Madal's only son."

Chapter Seven

Captain Blade looked intently from one anxious face to the other. Sam couldn't believe that he would agree to leave the village to its fate.

The captain shook his head. "Usiano, we came here to rescue your people. I will not sway from that purpose unless you say I must."

"And you will never hear me say that!"

declared the boy hotly. "My father is dead so I am now the chief. I am going to save my village."

"Then we'll stand by your side," said Blade. He turned to the pirates. "Won't we, men?"

"Aye!" came the stout reply.

"I can see that you have made up your minds," said Adisman. "I fear it will not be easy. There are at least thirty invaders, all armed with flintlock pistols."

"And we're fifteen with hearts of oak!" exclaimed Ned, standing tall. "We're not afraid of mercenaries. Let's take them now!"

Adisman shot him a glance. "You give me hope," he said. "But we must plan carefully. Let me get back to the village before I am missed. Do nothing until I return to you. By then I will have found out the best time for you to attack."

He disappeared into the undergrowth and soon they could see him slipping back into the shadows under the hut.

"While we wait we must decide *where* to attack," said Blade firmly. "Let's hear what our three young spies found out." He took a stick and drew a circle in the earth. "This is the village." He added some wavy lines on one side. "And here's Lake Laya. Where were the guards positioned, boys?"

Fernando pointed to the middle of the circle. "From where I was, I could see that there were plenty guarding the villagers here."

"And I saw many men walking up and down the forest boundary," added Usiano.

"But there was no one on the shore," Sam put in. "Some were in boats with the pearl fishers . . ."

"But surely they'll be gone by nightfall," said Charlie eagerly.

Usiano nodded. "It is impossible to find oysters at night, even by the strongest moon."

Blade pulled at the braids in his beard, deep in thought. "Then the lake would seem the best place from which to attack," he said.

"I do not think so," said Usiano. "A canoe would be noticed at once. Even the mercenaries know that – that is why they have no guards on the shore."

"Then we'll swim," said the captain firmly. "You four youngsters slip round and spy out the lagoon. Find a place where we can slip into the water unseen. Then report back to me."

Usiano led the way through the trees. "Keep close," he called over his shoulder. "It will be dark soon."

Sam remembered that night fell suddenly in the Caribbean and he didn't want to get lost in this tangled forest. The trunks were more twisted now and creepers hung down like tattered curtains, making deep shadows as the light faded. The ground beneath his feet became squishy with mud, but the trees and undergrowth were too dense for him to see the lake as they followed Usiano round its bank. They could hear the rough shouts of the mercenaries giving orders to the villagers.

They started past a bush that looked as if it was covered in white flowers, but when they brushed against the leaves, Sam realised that the flowers were butterflies.

They flew up into the air like snowflakes in a blizzard.

"Merow!" Sinbad leapt from Charlie's shoulder, batting mid-air at the fluttering creatures. He shot over the bush and they all heard a huge splash!

Charlie started forwards in alarm. "My poor boy!" she exclaimed. "I must rescue him!"

Sam pulled her back. "You'll be seen by

the men in the boats!" he warned. "Sinbad can take care of himself." As he spoke there was a loud miaow and the indignant ship's cat appeared at Charlie's feet, water dripping off his bedraggled fur. He hissed at everybody.

"Well, it's not our fault," said Fernando, keeping a safe distance. "You chose to go swimming."

"I hope no one heard him from the boats," said Sam.

Usiano listened hard. "I think not," he replied.

"You are a very silly cat!" said Charlie, wagging a finger lovingly at Sinbad.

"Not so silly," said Usiano to everyone's surprise. "Captain Blade wanted us to find a good place to swim to the village and Sinbad has found it. We can see the whole shore from here but remain hidden in the bushes until we slip into the water." He stopped to listen. "The boats are finishing for the day."

They parted the leaves and looked out over the lake. The exhausted villagers were pulling the canoes up onto the shore. The mercenaries lit torches that sent long shimmering lights across the dark water.

"Let's go back and tell the captain," said Charlie eagerly.

Fernando put up a hand. "Wait," he muttered. "I've thought of a problem. We know that the shore wasn't guarded during the day, but we have to be certain it's not guarded at night either."

"You're right," agreed Sam. "If we stay here a while longer, we'll find out."

Soon the forest was full of rustling and the cries of night animals. The full moon was reflected in the lake. A pair of glowing eyes appeared on a branch above Sam as some nocturnal creature came to inspect him and then darted away.

"There's still no one on the lake edge,"

said Fernando, pointing. "They don't expect any trouble from the water even at night. Now we can report what we've discovered."

Before they could move they heard angry shouts, and shots being fired in the forest beyond the huts. Sam pushed through the leaves and checked out the scene. The mercenaries were dragging some captives into the centre of the village. The captives were putting up a fight but they were outnumbered.

"I think some villagers have tried to escape," he reported. "They're being brought back. I hope we can make our attack before something terrible happens to them."

He got out his spyglass and focused on the scene.

"I was wrong!" he

gasped. "It's not villagers. It's Captain Blade and the crew. They've been captured!"

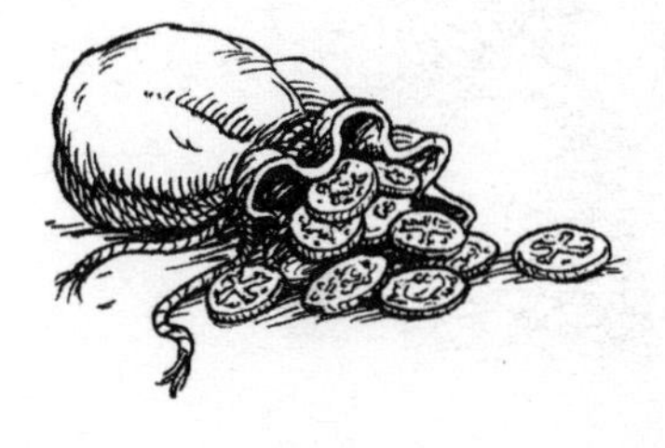

Chapter Eight

Sam snapped his spyglass shut. "The mercenaries have taken them all," he told the others.

"That's terrible!" cried Charlie, horrified.

"How could it have happened?" said Usiano. "Your crewmates were well hidden." He gave a sudden gasp. "It is my fault for alerting my uncle. Someone must have seen him come to us. I've put him in danger too. I have done a terrible thing!"

"You can't blame yourself," Sam told him.

"I was so desperate to free my people I did not think properly," said Usiano bitterly.

"We all knew the risks," said Fernando. "You did what you thought was best. And there is still something we can do."

Usiano looked at him with sudden hope.

"We must go to their aid." Fernando sliced the air with his dagger. "We're the only ones who can save them – and the village."

"And we are going to do it!" said Charlie fiercely.

But how? thought Sam. *It would be easy in a film. I could zoom round there in the Batmobile, or turn into Superman and fly to the rescue with my pants over my tights, but in real life I don't have superpowers.* He racked his brains for a plan that might work.

"My brave companions," said Usiano. "I am honoured that you are willing to risk your lives for my people. But four against so many . . ."

Miaow!

"Five," said Charlie, scooping up the damp cat.

"We're *Sea Wolf* crew," declared Fernando. "So we'll carry out the captain's plan. We'll swim to the village and take the villains by surprise."

"Usiano's right," said Sam. "We'll never overcome them on our own. I say we release our friends first. Then we'll be more evenly matched." An idea began to form in his head. "Fernando and I will swim across the lagoon," he went on, "while you three cause a diversion to keep the mercenaries busy."

"Wonderful, my friend," said Fernando doubtfully. "What should they do? Dance a hornpipe in front of them?"

"Course not," said Sam. "They'll make for the spider tree where the spirit lives."

Charlie nodded but a look of fear came over Usiano.

"You two will shout into the hollow tree," Sam went on excitedly. "That will sound as if something terrible is coming to get the mercenaries! As soon as they're running about panicking at the ghastly noise, Fernando and I can find our crewmates and free them."

"Then together we make an all-out attack!" Fernando's eyes sparkled at the thought. "I'm sorry I scoffed at your plan."

But Usiano was shaking his head. "I cannot disturb Hallucca."

Charlie put a hand on his arm. "Hallucca would want your people saved from those dreadful men," she said gently. "He'll be pleased we're using his tree to help them."

Usiano took a deep breath. "You are right," he said. "The spirit is on our side. He may even help us. We will do it."

"Fernando and I need to be in position by the time you get to the tree," said Sam. "We must leave straight away."

As he spoke, loud voices reached them from across the lagoon. They quickly peered through the bushes to see two mercenaries strolling down from the village towards the water's edge. The men sat on the shore and there was a flash of light as they lit pipes.

"They'll see you swimming," said Charlie. "You can't go now."

"We can if we go underwater," said Sam. "We just need something to breathe through. If only I had my snorkel . . ."

"Excuse my friend," Fernando said to Usiano. "He says strange things sometimes."

Sam pushed through the leaves until he had a good view of the bank beyond. "The men are looking this way," he reported to the others, "but the reeds will hide us as we get into the water. It's the swimming that will be difficult . . ." *Wait a minute,* he thought. *Reeds are hollow. We could suck air through them.* He scrambled back. "I know how we can swim all the way underwater!" he exclaimed. "This may sound a bit mad, but we can use reeds to breathe through."

"Then you won't be seen until you reach the village!" exclaimed Usiano. "That is not mad – it is wonderful. Come, Charlie and Sinbad, we must not delay."

They disappeared into the forest, slipping between the hanging creepers.

Keeping low, Sam and Fernando slid into the water and broke off a reed each. The men were still on the far shore, talking in low voices, and Sam was convinced that they would hear the snap of the stems, but to his huge relief nothing happened. He tried sucking in air through his reed.

"Works okay," he said quietly.

"We'll have to surface now and again to check we're going in the right direction," said Fernando. "It'll be impossible to see very far ahead once we're underwater."

"Too right," Sam replied. "We don't want to go round in circles all night."

He eased himself into the lake, making sure he made no noise. Fernando followed. Sam took a deep breath and sank below the surface, holding one end of the reed in the corner of his mouth and keeping his head to one side so that the reed stayed upright.

The lagoon was cold and dark. At first Sam could feel slimy weeds catching round his bare feet as he walked out from the shore. The bottom was sloping away fast so he kicked off and swam strongly, sucking hard to take a breath. Immediately his mouth filled with water and he surfaced, choking. Fernando came up behind him.

"You can't be lost already!" he whispered. "We've only just started!"

"Of course not!" spluttered Sam, "but I've just swallowed half of Lake Laya.

My brilliant reed idea wasn't so brilliant after all."

"It was," said Fernando, paddling beside him. "You must have set off too fast. I expect the reed was dragged back and it went under the water. Go slower and you'll be all right."

Sam looked towards the shore. He hoped no one had seen and raised the alarm. But all he could hear were the quiet murmurs of the pipe smokers.

He slid under the surface and swam with slow strokes. When he sucked at the reed this time, air filled his mouth instead of water.

It was eerie swimming in the dark lake. He felt something touch his arm and kicked hard to avoid it. *It's just a fish,* he told himself firmly, but he felt a chill of fear running through him. *What's the worst that can happen?* he told himself. *I get attacked by a killer oyster?*

There was a sudden movement in the dark water in front of him. Something huge was coming straight towards him, massive and menacing.

Chapter Nine

Sam surfaced quickly and gulped in air. He had the horrible feeling that a crocodile was lurking underneath him. He thrashed about, trying to make it impossible for the creature to grab him, hoping he wasn't alerting the men on the shore. He tried desperately to remember if you fought crocs off like you did sharks but his brain seemed to have frozen.

The water bubbled up right in front of him and he found himself staring at a large whiskered face that was gazing solemnly back. The creature was like a huge seal. It reached forwards and prodded him in the chest with its nose. Then it stared at him again and gave out a cry that sounded like a squeaky gate.

"What's that commotion?" came a harsh cry. The two mercenaries had come to the water's edge, silhouetted against the flickering torchlight.

Sam quickly disappeared under the surface. The huge creature dived with him. Now he had a choice. He was either going to be caught by the mercenaries or eaten by this monster. But the monster gave him a friendly nudge and Sam suddenly realised he knew what it was. He'd seen these giants on wildlife programmes. It was a manatee – and they were harmless! He was about to take a breath of air when he realised he didn't have his reed. Well he wasn't going to surface again, not with the men on the lookout.

He struck out for the shore. Just as he thought he was going to burst, he felt the bottom of the lake under his feet and reeds in front of his hands. He raised his head carefully. He was hidden by the tall stalks.

Fernando was already there, peeping through the rushes at the village. "Now to hide somewhere ready for the signal," he said in a low voice.

"Avoiding those two for a start," Sam murmured back, nodding at the pipe smokers who had sat down again on the shore.

Skirting a canoe, they made for the shadows under the nearest huts. In the flickering firelight they could see the tribespeople sitting slumped on the ground. They were picking listlessly at their food. More mercenaries, all with flintlock pistols in their hands, walked around them keeping watch.

"Get this lot down to sleep for the night," came a rough voice and a man strode into view. He had a belt full of weapons and a hard face with a stubbly beard. He turned to one of the guards. "I want them working the moment dawn breaks," he snarled. "Pearls don't fish themselves and we've got fortunes to make."

"Aye, aye, Rufus," answered the nearest guard. The rough man grunted and strode away.

That must be their leader, thought Sam.

One of the guards kicked out at a woman, sending her sprawling. "Sleep!" he yelled.

They watched as the tribespeople lay down on the hard ground and tried to make pillows with their hands.

"We can't let this go on," gasped Fernando. "They're treating them like animals. They're not even letting them sleep in their huts. I wish Charlie and Usiano would hurry up and make the tree speak."

Sam strained his ears but he couldn't hear any moaning noises from the spider tree. "They should have got there by now," he said. "I hope they're all right."

Rufus came striding back. "You four stay and guard this miserable lot," he called to the nearest of his band. "The rest of you come with me and get fed. Then I've got some target practice for you." He laughed horribly. "Pirates in a pen!"

Sam threw Fernando a horrified look. "We can't wait for Charlie and Usiano!" he gasped. "Our shipmates are about to be killed. But where are they?"

"He said pirates in a pen," said Fernando.

"He must mean the goat pen!" exclaimed Sam. "Our friends will be there."

Darting from shadow to shadow they made their way to the edge of the village where they'd seen the pen. They could hear goats bleating softly and, as they crept between the tall posts under a group of huts, they saw the small fenced enclosure lit by a spluttering rush light.

"There they are," hissed Fernando.

Their friends were huddled together amongst the goats, their hands tied behind their backs. The goats grazed around them, taking an occasional nibble at their clothes. Some guards stood at one end, guns in their hands, chatting in low voices.

Fernando set off on all fours towards the fence. "We must play at being goats," he whispered, carefully cutting a gap in the fencing with his knife. "Go slowly. We don't want them getting frightened and alerting the guards."

Sam followed him in, squeezing through the tiny gap, trying not to make a sound. The goats looked up curiously as the boys crawled towards them, then a few of them ambled forwards. Sam and Fernando froze, but the mercenaries were busy with their conversation. Even their shipmates had not spotted them.

A large animal with curly horns trotted

ahead of the others, its head down.

"I don't think it likes us!" mouthed Sam, steeling himself for a buffeting.

But the goat merely ambled to a halt in front of Fernando and began solemnly chewing his curly hair.

Sam stifled a chuckle as his friend struggled in slow motion to get himself free. They crawled slowly towards their shipmates through the jostling herd.

Sam could see the captain's buckled shoes just ahead but it was hard to push his way through the nosy animals without alerting the guards. And at any moment, the others would arrive with their belts full of ammunition, ready to shoot the trapped pirates. And what had happened to Charlie and Usiano? He swallowed down his panic and squeezed past a scrawny goat. At last he reached the captain. He tugged at the end of his ragged trousers. Blade ignored it.

He must think I'm just another goat! thought Sam.

"*Meh!*" he bleated loudly, giving the trousers another hard pull. "*Meh!* Down here. *Meh!*"

This time it worked. He looked up straight into the astonished face of his captain.

Blade crouched as if he was too tired to stand and Fernando slipped out his knife and got to work cutting the rope that was binding his hands.

"You all right, Captain?" came Ned's low, anxious voice. "Are you ill?"

The rope fell away and Blade flexed his hands but kept them behind his back. He stood up.

"I'm fine, Ned," he answered. "In fact I feel surprisingly care*free*." Keeping them out of sight of the guards he flapped his hands so that Ned could see the ropes had gone.

"Well I'll be a pilchard in a pickling pot!" whispered Ned. "That's a clever trick."

"Don't move!" hissed Sam, as Fernando began to saw at Ned's ropes. Ned pulled at his bonds, splitting them before Fernando was finished. Sam got to work on Ben. The pirates found it hard to hide their grins as they realised what was happening.

"Do nothing till we're all free," muttered the captain, his voice masked by the goats' low bleating. "Then we'll start with our guards here. Once we've overcome them and got their weapons we can take on the others."

The crew nodded, each freed man standing as if he was still bound.

Fernando slashed the last bonds. "All done, Captain," he hissed. "Ready to attack!"

"What's going on?" growled one of the guards suddenly.

Sam saw the man lean over the fence and peer intently at the pirates, holding up a flaring torch to light the pen. The *Sea Wolf* crew stood still, heads bowed.

"Don't move!" Fernando whispered to Sam. "With luck they won't spot us."

They stayed crouching among the goats but the glare of the torch spooked the animals, making them shy back. Now Sam and Fernando were caught in the light.

"What have we got here?" came a nasty voice. "Strange goats indeed!" It was

Rufus. He'd arrived with his band of mercenaries and they all had guns. "Stand up, boys, and we'll give you a quick end." Rufus raised his pistol and pointed it at Sam and Fernando. "And you can drop that knife!"

Fernando let his knife slip from his fingers.

Blade started forwards. Rufus fired, shooting the captain's hat right off his head.

"I'll go for your leg next," he said. "Let you bleed a bit before I finish you off." He laughed again, making a nasty growl in his throat. "By the time I've done, you'll be glad to die! Take aim, men."

Woooooooo!

The faint sound drifted out from the forest. One or two of the mercenaries looked up nervously.

"At last!" Sam whispered to Fernando. "Charlie and Usiano are going to save the day."

"They will have to make it a bit louder than that!" Fernando whispered back.

As he spoke the noise dwindled away.

"It's just an owl," snapped Rufus, keeping his eyes fixed on his captives. "Ignore it. We've got prisoners to shoot."

The men brought their guns up.

WAAAAAAAAOWWWWWW!

This time a bloodcurdling cry came ringing through the trees. The mercenaries froze, their fingers on their triggers. The noise was growing louder and louder, filling the air.

Sam felt his bones turn to jelly. He'd never heard such a terrifying sound in his life. It couldn't be Charlie and Usiano. Had the pirates escaped being shot only to face something much worse coming from the jungle?

Chapter Ten

The guards whipped round, pointing their guns at every shadow as the dreadful sound pierced their eardrums. Others came running to their leader, trembling with fright.

In the distance Sam could hear the villagers begin to wail the name of their spirit. "Hallucca! Hallucca!"

"Is it a demon?" asked a mercenary

fearfully.

"I'm not waiting to find out," said another.

"You're right. We should get out of this accursed place," muttered a third. "Let's grab the pearls and go."

"Stay where you are!" yelled Rufus, pointing his pistol at him. "You're going nowhere."

WAAAAAAAAOOOOOOWWWWWW!

The horrible cry came again. Sam could see that some of the pirates were looking around, anxious expressions on their faces.

"Has hell opened and let the devil out?" muttered Ned.

What is it? thought Sam desperately. *Could it really be Hallucca?* He put his hands over his ears to block the sound and then he suddenly remembered that he'd heard it before – not so loud or so deep, but it was definitely the same cry.

"It's Sinbad!" he whispered to his

crewmates. "We told Charlie and Usiano to make a diversion so we could free you."

"And they have, by Orion's Belt!" declared the captain. "Get ready for my order to attack."

The goats were bleating in terror at the strange sound. They charged at the fence in panic, sending it crashing to the ground, and galloped past the invaders. Some of the guards started running away, horrified looks on their faces.

"Come back, you yellow-bellied dogs!" yelled Rufus, firing wildly at them.

As soon as his back was turned, the captain leapt into action.

"CHARGE!" he roared, snatching up a broken fencepost.

The pirates threw themselves at the mercenaries, tearing up sticks and knocking the enemy aside. Ned laid about him with his huge fists and Sam and Fernando kicked and punched anyone in reach, sending pistols flying from their captors' hands. The mercenaries were too terrified by the dreadful wailing to stand and fight. They cowered back, gibbering. Rufus stood alone, turning his gun first on his own men and then on the pirates.

Blade advanced on him. The leader of the mercenaries now aimed his weapon at the captain's heart. His finger was on the trigger but Blade was too fast. He swung the wooden post, sending the evil man sprawling unconscious onto the dusty ground.

"Arm yourselves, men," he yelled, picking up Rufus's pistol.

The pirates snatched up the fallen weapons and began herding their guards together, tying their hands with the ropes that had once bound them. They marched the men to the centre of the village, Blade dragging Rufus along by the scruff of his neck.

Usiano's people had gathered round the fire, quavering at the fearful sound that was still coming from the forest. But, at the sight of the defeated invaders, their faces lost their terror and hope began to flicker in their eyes. Then they recognised the captain.

"Our friend!" called a woman carrying a baby.

"From the sea!" cried another.

Blade stared at the captives huddling

together on the ground. "You will not have the punishment that you would have given us," he told them sternly. "Indeed you will be guests on our ship – until we leave you on the next uninhabited island we find. Then you can do your own work for a change."

The mercenaries swore and pulled at their ropes but quickly fell silent when the pirates shook their pistols at them.

At last the howling stopped and Charlie burst out from the forest and ran to Sam's side.

"I see our diversion worked," she whispered to him.

"Sinbad deserves a whole bucketful of fish!" Sam whispered back.

"Don't worry," said Charlie with a grin. "I gave him a feast of fish from the lagoon before Usiano and I came back to help."

"It's time to put this village back to rights," declared the captain. "Where's

Usiano? He is your leader now."

"You are wrong, Captain!" came a harsh cry. "*I* am the leader now."

Adisman appeared. He had Usiano in a tight grasp and a knife pressed to his neck.

"I don't understand, Uncle," said Usiano, his words coming out in short, half-strangled bursts. "Are the mercenaries making you do this?"

"Weak, stupid boy," snarled Adisman. "You are just like your father. It was I who found Rufus and invited him to come here with his men. I drugged the villagers on watch so that the people were defenceless."

"It all makes sense now," said Blade, stepping towards him. "You told these men exactly where we were. You betrayed us – and your own kin."

"Do not come any closer!" Adisman's eyes were wild. He pressed the knife into Usiano's skin and a trickle of blood appeared. The villagers moaned in terror. Usiano stood stock still, not making a sound.

"Take one more step," snarled Adisman, "and I'll cut his throat!"

Chapter Eleven

Usiano's eyes were wide with fright as the knife pressed into his skin.

"I must congratulate you, Captain Blade, for getting this far," sneered Adisman. "I am so sorry that your little plan has not worked. Put down your guns."

"By Satan's breath, you are despicable!" growled the captain, raising his gun. "Let the boy go or I will shoot you."

"I will have slit his throat before you can pull the trigger," laughed Adisman.

"Do not hesitate because of me, Captain." Usiano managed to spit out the words. "I am willing to die to save my people!"

"Bravely said!" cried Blade. "But I am not willing to let you!" He dropped his pistol on the ground and turned to his crew. "Put down your guns."

"Untie these men," demanded Adisman.

"You see we are at your mercy, Adisman," said the captain calmly as the pirates began to free the mercenaries. Rufus was coming round now, and kicked out as his ropes were loosened. "Why don't we get together and try to find a peaceful solution to this terrible business before more blood is shed."

Sam gawped at the captain. Had he gone mad? Anyone could see that Usiano's uncle wasn't going to sit round a camp fire and have a chat about his plans!

Adisman curled his lip. "A peaceful solution?" he growled. "Never! You are all in my power now."

"At least explain to us why you have done this," the captain went on. "I have to admit, you outwitted us all."

Then it came to Sam. Captain Blade was trying to keep the evil man talking. He was playing for time – probably hoping that some of his men would be able to think of a rescue plan. Sam glanced around. It looked hopeless. All his crewmates were standing like statues, not daring to move a muscle. Unless Adisman went on talking for ever, it looked as if they were all doomed.

Adisman thrust his captive nephew at two of the mercenaries, who grasped the boy's arms tightly. "I did it because *I* should have been the rightful leader," he said, thumping himself on the chest. "My brother may have been older than I, but he was soft and weak. That is no good for a chief."

"He was not weak!" Usiano said through gritted teeth. "He was kind and his people loved him for it!"

There was a murmur of agreement amongst the villagers at Usiano's words.

"Silence!" screeched Adisman. He waved his knife at them. Its sharp blade glinted in the firelight. "Do you want to see this foolish boy die in front of you?"

Sam could see Usiano pressing his lips together to keep in his boiling rage.

"Of course I knew my brother would not see things as I did," Adisman went on with a nasty chuckle, "so I gathered together a band of desperate men who would do anything for the promise of riches."

"Desperate?" laughed Rufus, who had regained his swagger. "We're just doing our job – and being paid handsomely for it!" The other guards nodded, some firing bullets into the air, making the villagers cower.

Sam realised that no one was looking his way. The mercenaries were full of themselves, forgetting how easily they'd been overcome. This was his chance to try and slip away. He could race back to the *Sea Wolf* and bring reinforcements. No – there was no time, and anyway he'd be sure to get lost in the forest, which wouldn't help anyone! But he'd have to think of something – everybody stood more chance if he was free.

He caught a glimpse of a domed tent behind him. It was decorated in feathers and shells and the spidery tree emblem hung above the door. Sam remembered it now. They'd seen it when they'd been spying on the village. It belonged to the shaman.

The entrance was not far away – and Ned was standing in front of him. If Sam moved slightly to the side, the pirate's huge frame would shield him from sight. He could slip into the tent.

Then what? Sam's stomach lurched painfully as he realised that he had no idea what to do after that. But he knew one thing. Everyone was depending on him to save their lives.

Chapter Twelve

Adisman paced round the fire like a villain in a film, enjoying every moment as he told the pirates how clever he'd been. "The mercenaries I chose were well trained," he went on, his eyes gleaming. "It took them only a few moments to have the whole village at their mercy."

As he boasted about his evil actions,

Sam crept backwards, one slow step at a time. He scanned the faces of the mercenaries. When anyone glanced his way, he froze, moving on only when nobody was watching. At last he could feel feathers touching his skin. He must be at the tent entrance. He hoped it was empty. He slipped inside, into the dark, feeling his heart banging against his ribs. He almost gasped as he saw a row of pale ghostly faces with black eye sockets hovering in the air. But as he grew used to

the deep shadows he realised that the faces did not move. They were painted masks hanging on the wall. Gradually he could make out long wooden poles with strange carvings and elaborate robes decorated in oyster shells. His heart sank to his trainers as he realised there was nothing here but dressing-up clothes. They weren't going to help him save Usiano and the *Sea Wolf* crew.

Captain Blade was speaking now. "Think of the spirits that guard this place and its people, Adisman," he said, his voice low and calm. "You heard them calling from the spider tree just now. Aren't you afraid that they are coming for revenge?"

Adisman spat on the ground. "I laugh at the spirits!" he snarled. The villagers gasped. "Guns and knives hold the real power. If Hallucca is against what I have done, he can come here and tell me so this minute. As for now, I am chief and what I say goes!"

An idea suddenly shot into Sam's brain like an arrow. He couldn't make a real spirit turn up, but what if he could dress up in these weird clothes and a mask and appear with a dire warning? He was willing to bet his best football that no one had ever seen any spirits, so Adisman might just think it was Hallucca! Sam could come out of the tent, saying – in a deep mysterious voice – that Adisman was in big trouble. That would be the last thing he'd be expecting. With luck it would frighten the traitor long enough for the crew to overcome the mercenaries and free the village.

Then Sam realised his plan wouldn't work. He was too small. Adisman would realise it was just a boy behind the mask and would attack him with his knife.

If only I could make myself look taller, he thought. *In fact, I need to be so tall that I don't look human.* He felt round the dark corners for something to make him look tall – and nearly knocked over the two long decorated poles that were propped against the wall. He caught them just in time. His hands closed around deep notches in the wood. He held one up until a flicker of light fell on it from the fire outside. An eagle's face had been carved halfway up, its cruel beak curving down to a sharp point. The other pole was identical.

And now Sam knew just how he could make himself taller. He would use the poles as stilts! If he held the poles the other way up, he could rest his feet on the upturned beaks. But he couldn't get ready in the tent. There was nothing to climb on to help him on to the stilts – and he'd be much too tall to get out of the door once he was on them! So he'd have to sneak out and get among the trees to find a good platform for his stilt launch. Then he had a sudden thought. He was going to need his hands free so he could wave his arms menacingly and create maximum terror when he appeared. The trouble was, he only knew how to walk on stilts while holding on tight. But he had no choice. He ripped some strong leather ties from a tasselled tunic.

Holding the poles and a mask in one hand he draped two oyster-shell cloaks over his arm, almost groaning under the weight. Then he crept to the door and peeped round it. No one was looking his way so he slipped out, dragging the cloaks and sticks behind him. Keeping to the shadows, he ran to the shelter of the trees, and hid behind a bush near a low tree branch. Sam flung one cloak around his waist and tied it firmly. It hung in long folds on the ground. He pulled the other one quickly over his shoulders and then clambered awkwardly on to the branch. Soon he had the stilts strapped firmly to his legs. He checked that the cloak round his waist covered the stilts and finally placed the mask over his head. It felt stiflingly hot and he could hardly see through the narrow eyeholes.

Taking a deep breath, Sam launched himself off the branch and staggered forwards. He stumbled on the rough ground and almost fell, the ties cutting into his legs, but he steadied himself in time, his heart pounding. He could do this! How hard could it be for the best stilt-walker in Backwater Bay?

Sam gritted his teeth, stretched out his arms and strode with giant steps towards Adisman.

Chapter Thirteen

Everyone fell silent as the towering figure lurched towards them. Through the eye slits in the mask, Sam could see Adisman staring at him in shock.

It's working! he thought in amazement. Villagers were falling to their knees in front of him, but he had to make his crewmates understand that it was him under the robes and that this was their chance to overcome the enemy.

"It is a trick," blustered Usiano's uncle. "This is Nakili in his shaman robes. We've seen him a thousand times. We are not scared of him."

The villagers looked anxious and muttered in their language.

"You should not show such disrespect, Uncle," cried Usiano. He struggled against the grip of the man who held him. Sam didn't know if Usiano had guessed that it was him playing a trick or whether he believed it was truly Hallucca. Whichever it was he knew the boy would do everything he could to save his people.

"Why not?" Adisman spat out the words. "He is just an old man."

"That is not Nakili," Usiano went on. "See how tall he stands. Our shaman is old and bent now, with many winters behind him, and this figure is much taller than any human. That is no mortal man."

"It is a trick, I tell you!" snarled his uncle. Horrified, Sam saw him raise his knife and step towards him. "We'll soon see how the shaman bleeds."

"The spirits will not forgive you," came a quavering voice and an elderly villager came out of the crowd.

"Nakili!" gasped Adisman, dropping the knife. His glance whipped from Sam to the shaman and back again. "But it can't be ... If you are here ..." A look of horror spread over his face. He gulped as if his mouth was suddenly too dry to speak. "If you are here," he croaked again, "then who is that?"

Sam stood wobbling on his stilts, making the oyster shells on his cloaks rattle threateningly. He slowly raised one arm and pointed at the traitor.

"Adisman!" he shouted in as deep a voice as he could manage. "You have done great wrong to your people." He hoped the mask would help make his words sound menacing. But, suddenly, he realised he'd made a terrible mistake. He broke into a cold sweat under his costume. He shouldn't be addressing Adisman in English. The Layakati spirits would surely speak in their own language. The game was up!

Then he saw Charlie looking at him, the ghost of a smile playing round her lips.

"It's Hallucca!" she cried. "He has taken human form and is possessing the robes. He warned us from the forest and now he has come to free his village from the oppressors. You told him to show himself, Adisman, and he has answered your call!"

"Hallucca speaks in the language of the mercenaries so that they understand they have angered him," said Usiano, turning to his people.

Sam took his cue. "INVADERS BE GONE!" he bellowed, waving his arms.

"Hallucca!" the villagers took up the cry. Louder and louder they chanted. "Hallucca! Hallucca!"

The mercenaries were all gawping at Sam. Some had let go of the pirates that they were supposed to be guarding and were sidling away from the ghastly apparition. Sam could see Blade and the others moving together, and the villagers were following their lead. As they chanted they marched towards their enemies, fists punching the air, feet pounding menacingly on the ground. It was too much for the mercenaries. They dropped their guns and fled into the forest. Adisman gave a despairing cry and snatched up a pistol.

"Keep away from me, Hallucca!" he screeched, aiming the gun at Sam.

Sam realised he was going to get shot! He tried to step sideways but lost his balance. Now he was tottering towards Adisman. The more he tried to change course, the faster he went. He was out of control.

Adisman backed away, his eyes wide with fear. "Stop!" he shrieked, dropping his pistol. "Don't hurt me, Hallucca!"

Sam knew he couldn't stop even if he wanted to. It was as if the stilts had a life of their own. He was almost sprinting at Adisman now. He toppled forwards like a felled tree. He saw Adisman's terrified face getting closer and closer and then . . . *thud!* Sam hit the ground. It seemed surprisingly soft and it grunted.

Sam's mask had been knocked sideways and he couldn't see a thing. He fought to pull his arms free of the cloaks but he was just getting himself even more tangled. Strong hands grabbed him and he wriggled away furiously, convinced that Adisman was attacking him.

"By the stars, Sam," came a familiar voice in his ear. "You don't have to fight me."

Suddenly the mask was pulled away and he was staring into Captain Blade's grinning face. Fernando raced over to help and at last Sam was free of the robes and stilts. Adisman lay underneath, gibbering in terror.

"So that's what I landed on," said Sam, struggling to his feet.

Ned grabbed the traitor and had him tied up in a flash. "He won't be causing any more trouble," he said with satisfaction.

Sam looked round. Usiano was being welcomed by the delighted villagers. Charlie had Sinbad in her arms and Fernando was rounding up the goats.

"I don't understand," said Sam. "Where are all the mercenaries?"

"They ran off like cowards," laughed Ben. "Shame, I was looking forward to finding a nice barren island to maroon them on."

Everyone turned in alarm as shouts reached them from deep in the forest. They could hear fighting and gunshots. Wielding their cutlasses, Ned and Ben set off to see what was happening, but before they had reached the village boundary they were greeted by Harry Hopp and a

band of grinning pirates. They had the mercenaries tied up in a line behind them.

"Stap me," said Harry. "Shame we didn't leave the *Sea Wolf* sooner to come and find you. Looks like we've missed the fun. Though we did have a nice little fight with these bilge rats on the way. Know anything about them?"

While Blade told their tale, Sam gathered up the robes and the carved poles. He was horrified to see that one of them had a big crack in it. He took them over to the shaman. "I'm sorry for taking these without permission," he said, "and for the damage."

The old man beamed at him. "Hallucca will forgive you. You have done a great thing." He turned to listen to Usiano, who now stood on the steps of his father's hut, speaking to his people in their own language. Nakili gasped.

"What is it?" asked Sam. "What is he saying?"

"He says he is now their chief because his father is dead," said the shaman. "But he is wrong."

"Isn't he the chief then?" asked Sam. "Surely Adisman's not chief, is he?"

"No indeed," said Nakili. "Quickly, come with me. I hope we are not too late."

He led Sam away to the far edge of the village where a small hut stood on high poles. The door at the top of the steps was fastened shut with ropes.

Nakili pulled himself slowly up the steps and tugged at the ropes. Sam joined in, wondering what could be inside that was so important. At last the ropes fell away and he rushed in.

A man lay on the ground. He had a deep cut on his arm and the floor around was dark with blood. There were more cuts on his legs and his face was badly bruised. He lay with his eyes closed, not moving.

"Adisman threw him in here and left him to die," said Nakili, bending down and touching the man's face. "He could have had him killed straight away, but no, he wanted him to suffer. It is Chief Madal."

Sam stared down at Usiano's father. He hardly dared ask the next question. "Is he alive?"

Nakili turned his rheumy old eyes on Sam and then he smiled. "He lives."

Sam raced down the wooden steps of the hut.

Usiano was standing in front of his people, looking very sad as a feathered headdress was brought towards him. Sam could see he was about to be made chief of the Layakati.

"Usiano!" he yelled. "Stop!"

Usiano swung round in surprise and stared at him. Then his gaze went past Sam and his mouth dropped open in astonishment. He began to sprint towards the hut. Sam turned to see Madal, leaning heavily on Nakili, reaching out a hand towards his son.

Chapter Fourteen

Sam, Fernando and Charlie stood with Usiano on the deck of the *Sea Wolf*. The mercenaries and Adisman were locked securely in the hold and the crew were making ready to set sail. Captain Blade joined them and put his hand on Usiano's shoulder.

"I was right to trust in the spirits, Captain," said Usiano with a smile. "They brought you to me and I will be forever thankful."

"I will always help a true friend," said Blade. "But now we have some 'rubbish' in the hold that I'm eager to be rid of, so we'll away."

He strode off to take the wheel.

"Thank you for that wonderful feast last night, Usiano," said Charlie.

"You are the ones who should be thanked," said the boy. "You rescued my people and I want to give you these." He handed them each a large shining pearl from a box. "There is one for every member of your crew. You will see that they get them?"

"We will treasure them always, my friend," said Fernando, taking the box.

"I hope your father is better quickly," added Charlie as Usiano climbed over the rail and down to his canoe. He picked up his paddle and pushed away from the *Sea Wolf*.

"Nakili will see to that," he called up to them. "I thank Hallucca that my father is still alive to lead his tribe . . . and I thank you, of course."

They waved until his canoe was out of sight.

Sinbad strolled down the deck.

"Oh, my precious boy," cooed Charlie, ferreting in her pocket. "You must have a treat for being such a hero."

Sinbad sat down and opened his mouth, ready to sing.

"Belay that!" cried Captain Blade from the wheel. "Until he can learn to sing a shanty, Sinbad will eat quietly like the rest of us."

Charlie grinned and tossed a fish head to the cat.

"That reminds me," said Fernando. "Before Usiano's arrow came, you were going to show us *your* trick, Sam."

"I did!" said Sam eagerly. "You know when I was pretending to be Hallucca on those . . ."

"Oh, so that was your trick," Fernando interrupted. "Falling over on top of people. Good one, Sam!"

Before Sam could reply there was a yell from Harry Hopp. "Fernando! Those sails won't unfurl themselves!"

"Aye, aye," Fernando answered, springing up the rigging.

Sam sighed and looked at his pearl again. "My mum would love this," he told Charlie. "Shame I can't take it back with me."

"Pieces of eight!" came a squawk and before Sam knew what was happening, Crow had flown down, snatched it up in his beak and flapped up to the top of the mainmast.

"Oi!" cried Sam. He was just about to go after him when he felt a familiar tingling in his fingers and toes. He knew what that meant. He was about to be whisked back to the future and he couldn't let anyone see him disappear.

He dived behind Charlie. "If you can catch that pesky parrot, you can keep the pearl," he whispered as he was sucked up into the familiar whirlwind.

As he landed back on his bedroom carpet, he heard a resounding crash from downstairs.

"Sam!" came his mum's voice. "Take these wretched stilts away from your father. He's useless. I'll have no pot plants left at this rate."

Sam Silver, best stilt-walker in Backwater Bay, bounded down the stairs, grinning to himself. He'd have to teach his father to fall off his stilts properly. As long as he could find a handy villain to give him a soft landing!

The Sea Wolf
Charlie Fleetwood
Deckhand
Ben Hudson
Quartermaster
Sam Silver
Lookout
Ned Wainwright
Bosun
Harry Hopp
First Mate

CREW MANIFEST
Sinbad
Crow
Thomas Blade
Captain
Peter Craddock
Ship's Cook
Fernando
Rigger

Don't miss the next exciting adventure in the *Sam Silver: Undercover Pirate* series

The Treasure Map

Available in August 2013!
Read on for a special preview
of the first chapter.

Chapter One

Sam Silver stood in front of his class and held up his ancient gold doubloon. Their teacher had asked them to bring in the oldest thing they could find for their history lesson, and his coin was three hundred years old. If that wasn't history, then what was?

"This is a Double Eagle doubloon," said Sam eagerly. "It's really ancient and it used to belong to my great-great-lots-of-greats-grandfather, who was a pirate."

There was a gasp from the class but Sam could see his teacher looking doubtful.

"Did your parents tell you that?" asked Miss Elliott.

"No," said Sam. "It got washed up on the beach in a bottle, but I know it belongs to my family because there was a letter with it that explained everything."

Someone tittered near the back.

"It's true," insisted Sam. "I know because . . ." He stopped. He realised he couldn't tell the class anything else about his special coin. There was no way he was going to let out the doubloon's great secret – that it could whisk him back in time to the decks of the pirate ship *Sea Wolf* where he served as lookout boy under Captain Blade, the boldest buccaneer to sail the Caribbean Sea. Time-travelling undercover pirates can't tell anyone about their plundering adventures.

"Because?" prompted Miss Elliott.

"Er . . ." Sam said at last, feeling a bit embarrassed. "That's all I can say."

"Well, it's the oldest object today," said his teacher kindly. The bell rang for the end of school. "Homework, everyone!" she called over its chimes. "You brought in some very interesting historical items and now you're going to write stories about them. I want you to imagine you're living back in the time of your object."

Sam raced home to the flat above his parents' shop – The Jolly Cod, Best Fish and Chips in Backwater Bay. He'd had a great idea. He bounded up the stairs to his bedroom, threw off his school uniform and pulled on his tattiest T-shirt and jeans. Then he tipped the coin out of his backpack. He was going to have some pirate fun with his friends back in 1706. After that he could write it all up for homework and not even miss tea. That was the clever thing about the doubloon. No time ever passed in the present when he was off buccaneering.

He spat on the coin and rubbed it hard on his sleeve. "*Sea Wolf*, here I come!" he declared.

He felt the room begin to spin. The next moment he was pulled off his feet and tumbled round and round as if he'd been hoovered up in a giant vacuum cleaner. He braced himself for the landing. *Bump!* He was sitting on the wooden floor of a little storeroom, which was gently rocking. Awesome! He was back on the *Sea Wolf*.

Sam scrambled to his feet and gathered up the belt, jerkin and spyglass lying in the corner. His pirate friend, Charlie, always put them ready for him. She was the only other person in the world who knew that he was a time traveller – she'd seen him appear out of thin air once so he'd had to tell her the truth. It had taken some explaining but she'd understood, and now she helped to keep his secret.

Eager to see his crewmates, Sam sprang up the steps to the main deck and burst out into the hot Caribbean sunshine. The ship was moored in a bustling port where men were carrying crates and rolling barrels along the quay. There was an unpleasant smell of rotting fish wafting across the ship. To his surprise the *Sea Wolf* seemed empty. He felt a shiver of worry. Where were his crewmates? Then a deep voice hailed him from the foredeck.

"By the Great Bear, it's Sam Silver!" A tall pirate in a tricorn hat was leaning over the rail above him, weapons gleaming in the belts across his chest. His bearded face was wreathed in smiles.

"Captain Blade!" exclaimed Sam in relief. "Where is everybody?"

"Shore leave, lad," the captain called down. "Well, all except Peter. He's in the galley doing some cooking. The last fish pies he made were so hard we could have used them in the cannon. I thought he'd better stay on board and practise his pastry."

Sam realised that the nasty smell was coming from the galley, the ship's kitchen. He was glad he wasn't hungry. Even if Peter practised for a whole year he'd never produce anything that didn't break your teeth or send you running for the sick bucket.

"Permission to go ashore and find the others," said Sam eagerly.

"Surely you must have seen them when you came through the town," said Blade, puzzled. "Puerto Nuevo's not that big a place."

"Er . . . well . . . the thing is . . ." said Sam, racking his brains for an excuse. He couldn't tell the captain that he hadn't come through the town at all, but simply popped up in the storeroom from three hundred years in the future.

Every time Sam disappeared from the *Sea Wolf* to go back to the present, the crew believed that he'd gone to help his poor widowed mother on her farm, somewhere in the Caribbean. But he never remembered to have an excuse ready when he appeared on board without warning. And this time Charlie wasn't around to come to his rescue.

"I was in such a hurry to be with you all again," he said at last, "that I kept my eyes fixed on the ship."

"Well go and find your shipmates now," said Blade, ushering him towards the gangplank. "You've got time before we set sail."

"Thank you," said Sam, relieved that the captain wasn't asking any more questions.

"Ahoy, me hearty!" came a squawk. A green parrot landed on his shoulder and began to nibble his ear.

"Hello, Crow," said Sam, tickling him under his beak. "Did you miss me?"

"You can take that . . . bird with you," said the captain shakily.

Captain Blade was the bravest man

Sam had ever met – except when he was faced with a parrot. Charlie had heard it was because a parrot had pinched his toy cutlass when he was little, but all the pirates had different tales to tell. Everyone knew to keep the parrot away from Blade and pretend it was an unusually colourful crow.

"Aye, aye," said Sam smartly. He bounded down onto the quay and scanned the crowd, looking for Charlie and their friend, Fernando.

He walked past shops and taverns, skirting the fishing nets and lobster pots strewn over the cobbles. There was no sign of Charlie's bright bandana or Fernando's dark curly hair. Sam was willing to bet that most of the men he could see were pirates like them, who were acting like ordinary sailors but ready to vanish in an instant if the governor's soldiers came by. Then he spotted Harry

Hopp, the *Sea Wolf's* first mate, sitting at a table outside one of the taverns. Harry was playing cards, a tankard at his elbow and his wooden leg stuck out in front of him. A scrawny-looking man sat opposite him, his cards clutched secretively to his chest. Sam was about to call his shipmate's name when Harry jumped up, knocking his stool flying.

"Stormy seas?" squawked Crow, tucking his head into Sam's jerkin.

"Looks like it," said Sam as Harry pushed the table over, sending tankards and cards into the air.

Harry launched himself at the scrawny man and dragged him to his feet. "I won fair and square!" he yelled, a thunderous look on his face. "Pay up now or it's the last game you'll ever play."

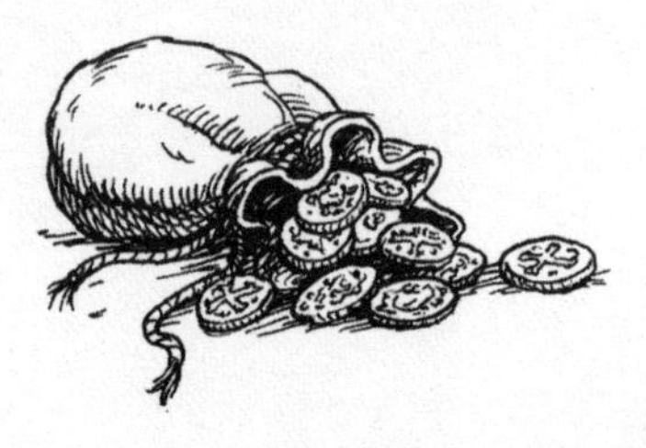